The blind and deaf walker of life, as lost and as burdened as all of us, suddenly stops; when, on countless occasions, falls, hitting the ground. Dies within, to allow repressed voice of Self speak at last. Sheds the layer of imposed identity and slowly moves forward, towards the light, encountering the quest to personal happiness.

To Eddie

For my children and the world – never forget the magic of love and kindness.

Always believe in your potential and potential of people around you

Aria

Aria Aimes

HEAR SILENT WHISPER

AUSTIN MACAULEY PUBLISHERS™
LONDON · CAMBRIDGE · NEW YORK · SHARJAH

Copyright © Aria Aimes (2018)

The right of Aria Aimes to be identified as author of this work has been asserted by her in accordance with section 77 and 78 of the Copyright, Designs and Patents Act 1988.

All rights reserved. No part of this publication may be reproduced, stored in a retrieval system, or transmitted in any form or by any means, electronic, mechanical, photocopying, recording, or otherwise, without the prior permission of the publishers.

Any person who commits any unauthorised act in relation to this publication may be liable to criminal prosecution and civil claims for damages.

A CIP catalogue record for this title is available from the British Library.

ISBN 9781528902014 (Paperback)
ISBN 9781528902021 (E-Book)

www.austinmacauley.com

First Published (2018)
Austin Macauley Publishers Ltd
25 Canada Square
Canary Wharf
London
E14 5LQ

Thank you for your encouragement in the simplest words and for opening the gate to the whispers of the worlds.

Table of Contents

Reason   **13**

  Whisper   *14*
  Heart   *15*
  Happiness   *16*
  Rules   *17*
  Universe   *18*
  Lifelong   *19*
  Yours   *20*
  Soul   *21*
  Light   *22*
  Inside   *23*
  Self   *24*
  Illusion   *25*
  Unreal   *26*
  Reality   *27*
  Morning   *28*
  Dream   *29*
  Song   *30*
  Selfish   *31*
  Night   *32*

Desired	*33*
Spirit	*34*
Unknown	*35*
Path	**36**
Waiting	*37*
Time	*38*
Professional	*39*
Split	*40*
Religion	*41*
Invitation	*42*
Message	*43*
Label	*44*
Flame	*45*
Grace	*46*
Facing Fear	*47*
Awareness	*48*
Cycles	*49*
Protection	*50*
Wisdom	*51*
Rising	*52*
Light Activation	*53*
Prayer	*54*
Inner Strength	*55*
Transcendence	*56*
Focused Intention	*57*
Ancestor Spirit	*58*

Flame	*59*
Infinite Abundance	*60*
Love	**61**
Whisper of Love	*62*
Reflection	*63*
Room	*64*
Tea	*65*
Fire	*66*
Angel	*67*
Image	*68*
Touch	*69*
Fear	*70*
Flow	*71*
Faith	*72*
Believe	*73*
Trust	*74*
Sleep	*75*
I Dare You	*76*

Reason

Whisper

Shh… Can you hear?
The tiny voice between the real and a dream
Whispers the truth once forgot
Asks you to stop
Can you stop?
Allow the voice to tell
The story of your own self
Does it match?
Can you feel?
Or does it sound rather unreal?

Heart

"Follow me," your heart says
"Follow me to the happiness
Where do you want to be?
I will take you there with me."
What is your purpose on Earth
Have you ever asked yourself?
Have you challenged status quo?
Or are you a silent quo pro quo?

Happiness

The state of your mind that allows the heart beat
The state of your soul that takes you high with it
To the places of your wildest dream
To the moments of your loudest scream
Where all is one, pure and innocent
When no longer mask is the way to descend
Young, beautiful, wild and free
Is who you want to be
No more acting, pretending to live
The life is here only once and will not forgive
The time when instead of you
The puppet acted according to rules.

Rules

Born to the ground of society
No longer me, no longer free
"Follow the rule," one wise man said
"Follow the rule and you will be safe."
Why to stand out
Why to rebel?
When you follow the rule
You always keep safe
Whose rule is that?
Why is it there?
Who has control
Over the universe?

Universe

The air, the earth, the water, the fire
Born to live to their own desire
Having their ways, making the play
In charge of life, born within them
How can a man happen to think
Taming the elements is a matter of blink?
We know so little, foolish to say
Taming is a part of a bigger game
What we forget life is unique
Should never be tamed so to speak
Should be left to grow wild and strong
Without being trapped for a lifelong.

Lifelong

"How long is a piece of string?"
One teasingly asks
How long is a lifelong
Is a different task
One lights up and happens to rise
One shadow never seeing the sun
Why is there a difference
Although both the same?
Who made this decision
Surely, it was not them?

Yours

Yours is the sky blue in a day light
Filled with the stars during a deep night
I am here standing, waiting to see
How you change yours into their will
Why do you not listen to whispers of old?
Why do you not follow desire of your own soul?

Soul

The first breath we take into this world
Allows the soul to enter the humanity scope
The soul knows well how it wants to grow
The society, however, has a different show
The soul is then framed, captured to live
Amongst the worlds that may never give
The release of her say talents and will
Forcing the soul to never fill
The purpose it had when coming with breath
The freedom it brought entering the Earth.

Light

Light watches you closely
Always there for you to see
Makes no difference for others
But a great one for me
Enters slowly but surely
Taking a step at a time
Have you learnt how to use it
Or is it still a deep mine?
Filled with greed of human race
Full of injustice and pain
How can you make the world a better place?
How can you help others to understand?
The light is there within each of us
The light is there, so do not make a fuss
Turn around, use your heart
Open eyes do not apart
Grow the light inside of you
Help me grow my light too.

Inside

Inside of us is the world
So beautiful and unique
The world of a dream
We all should live
It is our road map
A simple sign
Can you not see it?
Wake up, it is time
Time for you to walk lightly
On the surface of Earth
Be proud, be creative
Become your own self.

Self

Self was once born explicit in its shape
Self was free to perform the forms of its phase
Self has once met the other self
Staying close, self forgot the truth of its own self.

Illusion

What is normal and what not?
Can I follow certain code?
Would it matter if not mine?
No one ever gets a sign
We all puddle in a grime
Of low esteem that was left behind
How can we grow, flourish and bloom
When the example was set in lifeless gloom?

Unreal

Unreal is to hear the angel beside
The beauty sparks of blasting light
Walks beside you in the darkest of time
Leading slowly towards the growing light
You need to follow the whisper you hear
Allow it to lead you where others veer
That is how from strongly unreal
The angel leads to fulfil your own dream.

Reality

What makes a man to speak at free?
Is it the morning to meet and greet
Or is it a challenge from which to retreat?
The days that melt into growing blob
Or maybe the moments almost forgot
What makes a difference in the life one lives?
Is it the greyness of uncertainty
Or maybe a rainbow called abnormality?

Morning

"Take a step outside," the sun ray says
"Join me in a play which no longer takes
The growth of your soul into the vicious claws
Of limits and rims of those who think
They know better than you
Where to move you to
Those who always claim
You are no good for the game
Take a step outside of imposed thought
Smile, you are free to follow your own code."

Dream

I closed my eyes, sitting on a bench
The sun allowed the heat to overwhelm
My senses, my reasons, my cause and effect
I stopped to think I have to be perfect
I went on a journey led by sweet self
Unravelling the value of being myself
I saw magical land full of colours and joy
When I opened my eyes
All became obvious
Stop playing against your will
Start living the life of your dream.

Song

Sweet tune in my ears
Filling every vain
Takes me where I belong
Far from sorrow and pain
Takes me far on the wings
Borrowed from passing bird
Makes me to forget the walls of my iron cage
Moves to places where fantasy flows
Where no limits are placed on my unreal goals
Where the ownership belongs to me
And I can be free to sing the song
Of my destiny.

Selfish

You are rude, you are wrong
Why do you play this song?
Stop looking there
Stop wanting that
Do you not think you have enough?
What is wrong with you?
Can you not be
Like all the others
Who quietly follow the path
Laid there for them?
Do not be selfish
Fit into the frame.

Night

Twinkle, twinkle, little star
Makes me wonder who you are
'Who am I' question appears
When the twinkling carpet nears
The mundane existence of minions below
Why have we lost our inborn glow?
Why can we not proceed
To sparkle with joy amongst growing greed?
Why can we not release the restraints
Of limitations we all embrace
Upon our lives through negative thought?
Why can we not force once forgot
Beauty and joy sparkle and shine?
Why can we not follow the line
To show the stars, we are divine?

Desired

Close your eyes
Make a wish
Find the path to unity
This fine tune
Plays in you
Listen closely
To this tune
Takes you where
Infinite flame
Emanates with the glare
Takes you high
To the sky
With no limits
And no lies.

Spirit

What do you do at night
When the veil of darkness comes down?
Do you nurture your thoughts
Sieving the day that is now lost?
Do you taste the moments that were
Making your spirit flare?
Do you feel the ingrowing need
To release your spirit free?
Allow it to step into dance
With lifelong lasting romance.

Unknown

Step in and step out on the edge of unknown
Shyly moving closer, uncertain, lost and alone
Drawn towards the eyes, the touch, the mystery
Scared to be caught stealing moments from him
Overprotective hides them, still trying to understand
Is she allowed to forget and fall into the land
Of her dream, where no longer she
Is expected to fight
Where she can surround, dissolve and disarm
Where she can be certain to never be harmed
Only loved in a tune of a beating heart?

Path

Waiting

Fast tapping on the keypad
Forms the letters, into intriguing squad
Then the last ever look at the form
Of composed from the heart's inner flow
Hesitation on the verge of the need
And the question, 'what will happen if we
Press the button, sending out to the world'
What is inside of a protected scope?
What is true to the heart, so beloved?
Are we strong enough to expose
Our love and kindness to those
Who want nothing but to endorse?
Their position, although so fake
Having you to promise and make
What is there expected of you
Under threat of being removed
From the circle of so-called friends
But should they not really support and enhance?

Time

Tick-tock crocodile
It is time for me to smile
Send my love to the world
Hugging viciously yapping jaws
Changing bitter forms of words
Into flame of eager thought
To the passion filling veins
Swaying into sweet embrace
Of kind word spoken instead
Of complains' never-ending thread.

Professional

"Good morning, sir, how is your day?"
"Fine, thank you, and yours?"
"It is lovely, of course
Only the weather pain in the bum."
Oh, of course this is the only spam
In a perfect question and the reply
But what if there is no smile
Behind the mask of a man we speak?
What if instead is the suffering?
What if the pain seeks way to escape?
Will we ever attempt to change the shape
And be honest and true to the world
Making easier the change of the globe?

Split

Two lives to fulfil the requirement
One is yours, kept secretly in a fragment
Second shaped and formed to the outside
Ticking off every point of fake life
The civilisation imposed on us
Offering always new traps
To pick choose and sign for
Well done, you have accomplished the core
Of consumption never considered before
Welcome, you are in for
Maybe you should take more.

Religion

Easy excuse to set mind in a frame
Always done in the highest name
Of the god with a different face
Why is this so necessary to human race?
Can we not simply believe
In the kindness, helping hand and relief?
Why can we not live life and think
If we do harm to others, there will be a link
To harm being done to us
Kept as simple as a sign of a plus?

Invitation

Called by the voice deep inside
Changed by the factors which reside
Beneath the cautious layer of us
Thoughts of the world that encompass
Both beauty and human fatigue
Desire to plot never-ending intrigue
People whose light no longer shines
People who are better to close their mouths
When brining the factor of heartless stand
Who allowed them to speak, I cannot understand
Why is their voice so powered up?
Why are they not asked to shut up
And stop turning the world into hell?
There is so much beauty to fell
In love with causing the fine
Layer within each of us to clearly define
The reasons why we should advertise
The kindness and freedom as the best advice.

Message

Staring at the screen
Trying to make a message appear
Strong images of possible events
Came running fast, creating fear that sends
Your mind on a journey of unreasonable doubt
Making the worst options to come out
Forming the world of hopeless thought
Ensuring the failures are never forgot
But what if we thought of a fail as a step
So necessary in the evolution we get?
Through the life in the cautious spin
Falling and keep getting up is a win.

Label

The name once given
Creates a form
To the shapes, appearing around
Shapes changed by name do not cause a fear
Sticking labels around feels ever so real
Label is always theirs, never mine
I am the norm forming a spine
But what if the name was given to us
Making the change in the prestige of class?
Label is easy to stick
Searching the way to understand is unique.

Flame

Staring at the candle flame
Moving deeper, feeling the pain
Drawn towards the healing of life
Oh, dear light, help me survive
Take me up high to the mountain's top
Show me the image and allow to stop
Show generosity and collect the grief
Fill me in take my senses help to relief
Myself from the weight pulling me down
Snap the bonds of the miserable clown
Let me fly up into the sky
Let me show the world the widest of smiles
Feeling the power of overwhelming strength
Please let me fight injustice on Earth.

Grace

Beautiful lady passed me on the street
She was shy and lovely, willing to meet
The soul that takes her soul into arms
Slowly calming down the alarms
Of life in grief and human gore
Lady pleads to get some more
Warmth from the embrace of the other soul
The soul will come but soon after stroll
Leaving lady healed for the time
Teaching her tricks how to climb
Making lady clearly see
Life is a complex part of unity.

Facing Fear

Looked out of the shadows' zone
Majestic beast sitting on a throne
Made of the thorns causing the pain
Beast there sat in the restrain
A brave soul walked closer to see
Who hides behind the unknown tree
Moving closer, the soul felt the threat
But kept moving slowly with no regret
Soul wants to see clearly behind
Because the unknown makes our mind
To create the fear and the false shape
The fear then does not allow to escape
Grows over us, shutting inside
Builds the cages where you reside
Until the courage overtakes its way
Helping you openly say:
'No fear will ever shut me inside
I am the source of growing light.'

Awareness

Looking into the eyes of a little child
Whose innocence makes our spirit glide
Helping us to remind the time
When life was simple without the grime
At what point it happens that suddenly
We absorb the fear, thinking fondly
That this is only a passing trend
Not realising how this extend
Taking over the life of freedom and charm
Causing the damage and long-lasting harm.

Cycles

Spring, summer, autumn, winter
Four Earth seasons that inter
Different phases of the cycle, truth
Showing how to gently move
Between the natural matter of time
Something falls to let other climb
Only cycles let us move
Into a life of constant prove
Stay aligned to the flow
Fully understand and know
There is no reason to be attached
To the facts that are no longer matched
Pulling down and causing pain
Let it die to have again
Chance to plant the seed and grow
Incite the life's natural flow
It is your right to compose
Everything comes and everything goes.

Protection

In my dream, I saw him
The guardian of my vim
With the wings spread out wide
He watched my steps that always slide
Off the path, making me fake
He pointed out the points that break
The growth of light within me
Forcing my soul to agree
To restrains of reality
Damaging my personality
Commanded me to make a choice
And start to speak in my own voice.

Wisdom

Father of Old came down from his throne
Being shocked seeing the mourn
People lost, almost insane
Not knowing how to explain
What has been lost on the path
Why the humanity is in a wrath
Why did we all choose to step
Out of the concept to regret
Not learning the lessons history left
Allowing the leaders to make a theft
Of our freedom and peace on Earth
Why did we all allow ego the birth
The ego must be stopped before we get
Into position of no asset
When death and pain are only remained
And all the beauty lost and profaned.

Rising

Every time we fall, we should stand up again
There must always be something to gain
Do not allow yourself to stay
In the darkness, making you a prey
The world around is made by you
Rise back above the surface, moving through
The phases of growth, forming the strength
Take your time, do not look at the length
The healing takes to bring you back
On the surface of your personal track
Stronger and wiser form a plan
How to get back and throw a span
Showing the colours in your palette
This is how you fall and use a valet
To dress you up for crazy dance
Your life is back and you will take chance
To learn and fall, to rise again
No more, no less, always saying then.

Light Activation

What changed a man over the past decades?
Was it the need to succeed
Was it the thrive to discover the drive?
But did it all not make a man less
Has he not actually lost himself
Lost the light once shining so bright
Lost the guidance coming from inside?
What does a man has to do to see
Light is within him, waiting to spring
Shoot with kindness, warmth and more
Make a man revive his glow.

Prayer

When was the last time you stopped?
When was the time, when you forgot
To run, to need, to chase?
When was the time, when you embraced
Beauty of day a man next to you?
Is it no longer part of a rule?
Rule of the world around and inside
This is the best for us all guides
Guides through the hardship, struggle and pain
The one thing to do is to contemplate
Consider the weight of the matter once lived
Is it important or maybe you give
More than you should attention to thee
Blinding yourself to the aspects of how to be free
Ask the right question and you will receive
The tools you need to grow and succeed.

Inner Strength

Step one: you have the power to climb
Step two: the power is inside you
Step three: come dance with me
Step four: expect more
Step five: do not forget to smile
Step six: this is who you will be
Step seven: make on earth your heaven
Step eight: focus on your self
Step nine: there are no boundaries around
Step ten: become a free man.

Transcendence

No matter what happens to you
Remember to remain unmoved
Know who you are and do not change
Honour the inner force you have
It is there for a reason
Known to your own soul
Trust it, believe it, allow it to flow
Flow through you, freely giving steps
To find the way out of your distress
And when you are out from the darkest of dark
Feel the warmth of the rising sun
Close your eyes and allow the joy to run
Through your inner self, as it will no longer feel
Captured in a cage and restricted to rules
Breathe in deeply, slowly infuse
The magic you are
The magic that makes
You the most important part of the universe.

Focused Intention

Think about what you desire
Lift yourself, set the sight higher
No thought is wrong, no thought is a liar
You simply need to believe and admire
How shivers on your skin
How butterflies within
Show you the path
Where you will at last
Find the passion and love
When all listed above
Change from having a dream
To feeling good in your own skin.

Ancestor Spirit

White eagle flew above
Majestic shadow casts
Showing the way to find yourself
Connect to roots
Never forget the ancestors
Who, before you, walked in a pose
Watch them, remember those
Learn from the past and never repeat
The mistakes they, before you, lived
There are natural phases of growth
Stay away from the trap of owe
Make sure the lessons are learnt
Never forget what has been once said.

Flame

Rediscover a lost part of yourself
Follow a tiny flame, hide away
At the bottom of your heart
Where the active part
Plays the soul and inborn you
Never letting completely remove
The truth you were born with
The path you were shown with
Childish passion, naivety and believe
That the world is beautiful
And you will achieve
The goals of your life
Causing harm to none.

Infinite Abundance

Obstacles are being removed
Your heart and soul let loose
Spin and dance, in a life-loving trance
With spirit set free, not giving a chance
To cages set rules that were never yours
Climb over you restricting the move
Take a deep breath, ensure you have
The pleasure of joy with spirit support
Connecting to roots of your own truths.

Love

Whisper of Love

Shh… Do not disturb
Two souls have just met
They enter the ground
Of unknown land
They both are still shy
So fragile, divine
Will the world allow
The beauty to climb
Above the mundane
Where they can explain
The truths behind pain?
Can they remain simply alone
To understand the reason that thrown
Two souls together that cannot defeat
The power of growing between them energy?

Reflection

Once lost in his voice and depth of his eyes
The sea of his soul true to her own design
Both surrounded by the crowd of human grief
Afraid to take a step to feel a relief
Lost in her dream, she carries on
From the sunrise to inevitable fall
What happens to him, is he lost the same
Does he feel the struggle of a coming day?
Will they ever allow the moment that may
Change forever a portrait of the coming day?

Room

You walked into the room
Surrounded by crowd
Ever so important, sharing your smile
I was there amongst those
Who have meaningless pose
Watching shyly when you
Bravely entered the room.

Tea

Simple question for tea
Took us further than we
Would ever imagine to be
You took different approach
Changing the path of my soul
Shaking the ground inevitably
Ever since, step by step, moving closer
We have
Walked against our own rationality.

Fire

The sweet warmth of sparkling fire
Fills me in with my own desire
Slowly moves through the map of my skin
Expanding sensation from within
Taking control of what was unknown
Deeper, dissolving to lose control
Surrender to touch, to mystery
The growing illusion of harmony.

Angel

I closed my eyes for a moment
Allowing the thoughts which torment
Driving me crazy, moving to edge
Sliding slowly, soon to wedge
I saw you offering a helping hand
Pulling me out from the spin of the land
Showing the beauty of the world around
Lifting up from my stand on the ground
Moving closer, closing in arms
Infusing the joy, protecting from harms
I fell for you, my angel of love
We rise together always above
Aiming to climb the highest of heights
Together supporting our inner lights.

Image

You came to me at night in my dream
When generous sky shared a moonbeam
We walked together into the dark
Making each other glow and spark
You were holding mine in yours hand
We bravely stepped into the land
Of yet unknown but tempting zone
With no fear of being ever left alone
I gave you my heart, you offered yours
We will never be afraid of the closed doors
Supporting and giving the strength
We found each other, despite the length
Of time it took us to trust and believe
Although so hard to fully conceive
The soul has found its soulmate
This was a matter of their fate.

Touch

Sliding your fingers gently on my skin
Causing the storm of senses within
I surrender to you, lowering the guard
Revealing the strongest of all card
Please be gentle and protect from pain
I am armless and fragile, with open vein
You moved deeper under, becoming a part
Of my blood flow, confident, creating an art
Of love when no longer they
Take a part in an active play
It is purely just you and I
And the moment when we fly
Lifted high and above the known
Going deeper, we explore the zone
Of the world beyond reality
Giving way to our sensuality.

Fear

I walked past you on the stairs one day
You passed me and caused the ray
Of light to shine on me
Lifting the thought to set free
This was the time when I felt
I should not tight the belt
Around my neck and restrict the flow
Of the inner power that makes me glow
Since that day, I promised to take
Different path which is no longer fake
It is mine from the start to an end
I will no longer change in order to blend
I am me and me I am
This was time when I became a dame.

Flow

The nature has her natural flow
Of rhythms which throw
The need of change to human mind
Stopping them from being blind
Follow the path the nature sets
Listen to instincts, avoid the threats
Return to the path
Adjust the maths
Set yourself free
And no longer be
In owe to the people not making you grow
Listen to your natural call for the flow.

Faith

I have faith in you
Colour the world with value
Of love and light, kindness and smile
Take a palette and go wild
Use all the colours, mix them and match
I want you to live, not to be trapped
Set yourself free and fly above
The mundane and the greyness of life
Most people live getting sad
Question the orders, avoid the trap
If you obey your inner rules
The life will remain forever yours.

Believe

I believe in you
Do you believe in me too?
Please listen to the words I say
Please understand the pain that may
Stop me from enjoying the life
I promised to love you as your wife
But I no longer can live in a trap
I am sorry, please let me recap
The road we walked together was yours
You closed in front of me all of the doors
That were making me flower and bloom
I surrounded you and wore a costume
I can no longer move on the path
That makes me feel in growing wrath
I want to love, glow and shine
I want to move where the world is mine.

Trust

You covered my eyes
I let go of all shies
Giving you the life of mine
Allowing light to align
With the rhythm of heartbeat
Ensuring we both meet
On the path of truth and trust
There is no reason we should adjust
Our selves to self of you
If there is no match, it is better to drew
Apart, releasing the way
Letting loss of what no longer pay
Towards the growth of you and me
It is better to separate rather than be
Stuck in the cage of false realm
Giving the grief to overwhelm
The life of yours and life of mine
I wish you all the best, please be free and shine.

Sleep

I want to close my eyes
Feeling safe in your embrace
Please let me sleep
Hold me close, protect from pain
No more tears, no more grief
Let me sleep and find relief
Allow me to recover my strength
When I wake up, we move a full-length
Forward to laugh and smile in wild
Feeling free and happy like a child.

I Dare You

I dare you to love me day in and day out
I dare you to accept all imperfections of mine
I dare you to dance with me in a joy of the sun
I dare you to cry with me when tears cannot stop to run
I dare you to accept the challenge of life
I dare you to live surrounded by light.